HOW TO CLEAN A HIPPOPOTAMUS
A LOOK AT UNUSUAL ANIMAL PARTNERSHIPS

Steve Jenkins & Robin Page

Houghton Mifflin Books for Children • Houghton Mifflin Harcourt
Boston   New York   2010

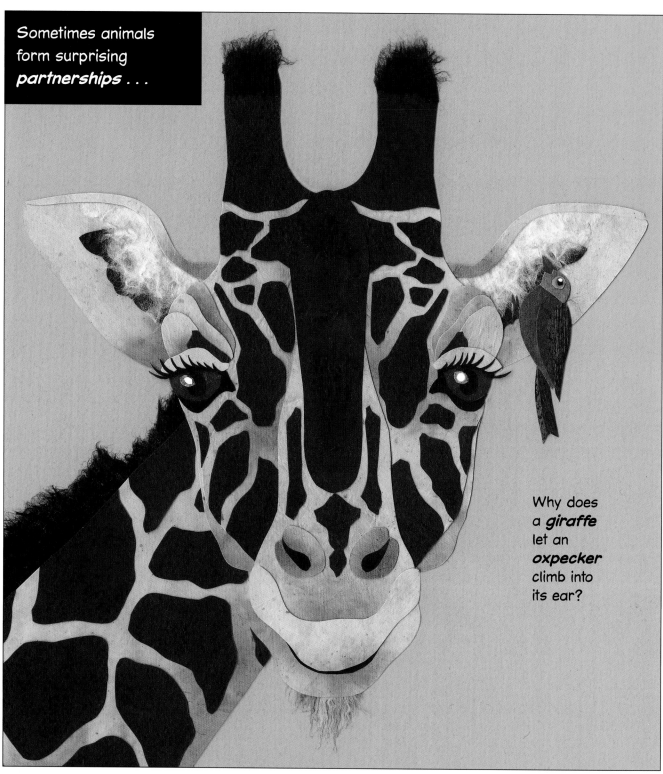

Sometimes animals form surprising *partnerships* . . .

Why does a *giraffe* let an *oxpecker* climb into its ear?

Why does a *crab* wave an *anemone* like a pom-pom?

Why do a *coyote* and a *badger* team up?

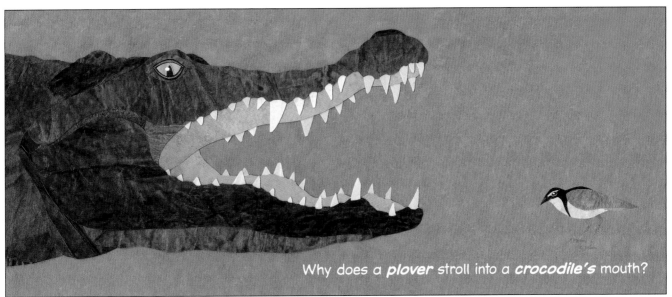

Why does a **plover** stroll into a **crocodile's** mouth?

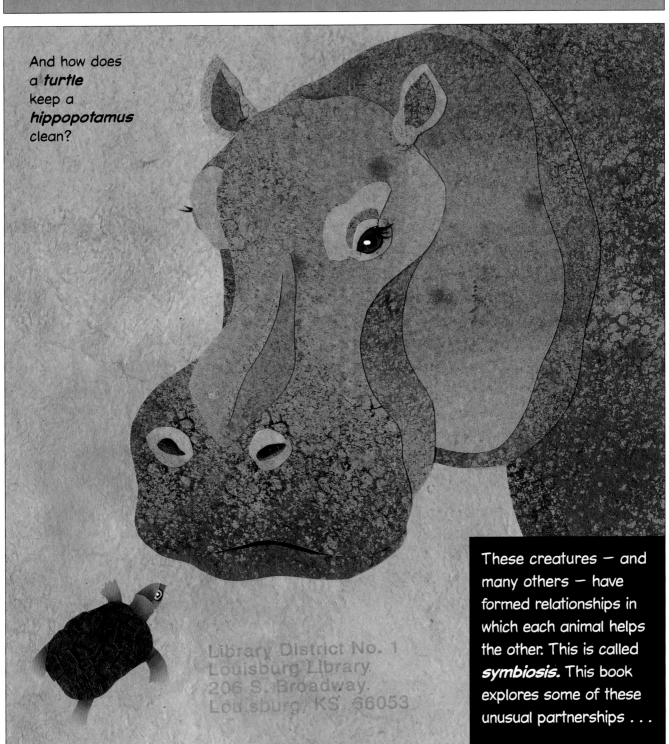

And how does
a **turtle**
keep a
hippopotamus
clean?

These creatures — and many others — have formed relationships in which each animal helps the other. This is called **symbiosis.** This book explores some of these unusual partnerships . . .

On the African savannah, **grazing animals** must lower their heads to eat, which can make it easier for a **predator** to sneak up on them.

Three different animals have found that feeding together makes them safer: each detects **danger** in a different way.

The **zebra** has excellent hearing. It stays alert for the sound of danger.

The **wildebeest** has an acute sense of smell. If the wind is blowing the right way, it can sniff out a nearby predator.

The **ostrich,** the tallest of the three, has sharp vision. It frequently lifts its head and looks around.

The **cattle egret** is a long-legged bird of the African grasslands. **Grasshoppers** are one of its favorite foods.

This egret hitches a ride on a **waterbuck,** a large antelope.

As the waterbuck grazes, its hooves stir up grasshoppers hidden in the **grass.**

The **insects** fly up and the egret swoops down and nabs them.

The egret helps the waterbuck by warning of **danger** with a loud call.

LOOK OUT! That lion is getting too close for comfort.

The *giraffe* can keep most large predators at bay with sharp hooves and a powerful kick...

...but like many wild animals, it is tormented by tiny ticks and other skin *parasites.*

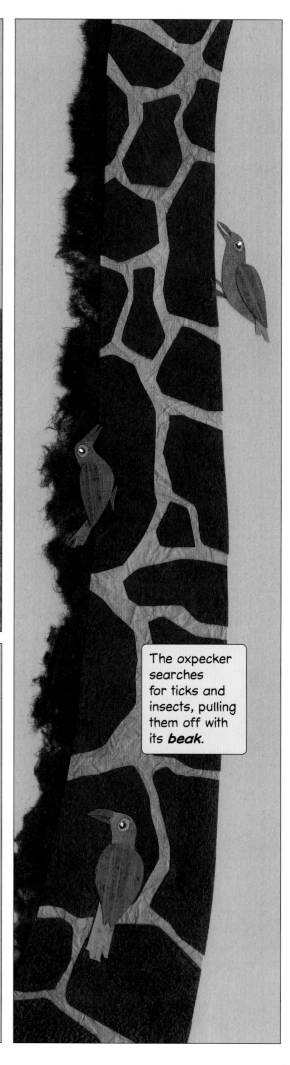

The oxpecker searches for ticks and insects, pulling them off with its *beak.*

The *oxpecker,* also known as a *tickbird,* eats ticks and insects.

The oxpecker will **warn** its host of approaching predators. If its giraffe has fallen asleep, the bird wakes it with loud shrieks and flapping wings.

The giraffe lets the bird pick off pesky *parasites* wherever it can find them.

HAVE BEAK, WILL TRAVEL.

Giraffes aren't the only large animals that form partnerships with the oxpecker.

Here, an oxpecker de-bugs a **rhino.**

Another helps out a **deer.**

And a third inspects an **African buffalo.**

These oxpeckers take a **song break** from **zebra** cleaning.

All of these large animals benefit by having fewer *parasites,* while the birds get to feast on their favorite **food.**

The *Egyptian plover* is sometimes called the *toothpick bird.*

The plover feeds on scraps of *meat* that get stuck in the teeth of the *Nile crocodile.*

The crocodile will *devour* any animal it can catch, but it won't eat a plover. In return for a tooth cleaning, it lets the little bird come and go freely.

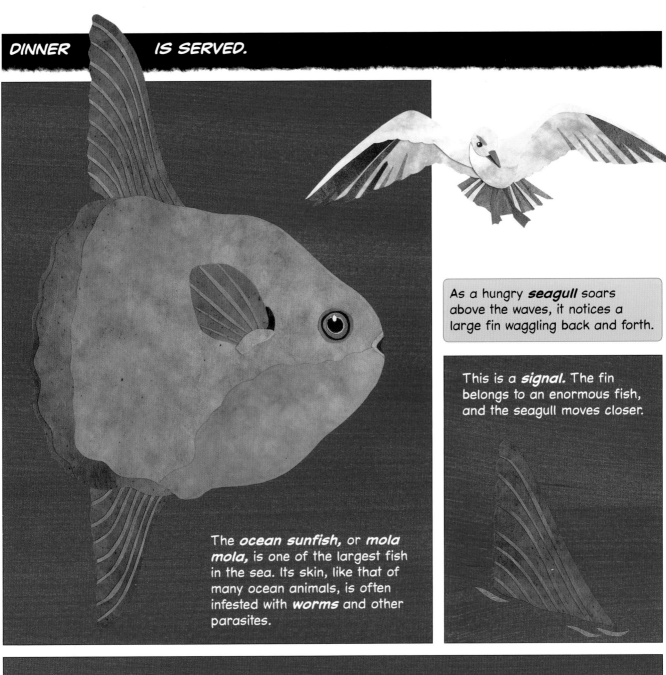

As a hungry *seagull* soars above the waves, it notices a large fin waggling back and forth.

This is a *signal.* The fin belongs to an enormous fish, and the seagull moves closer.

The *ocean sunfish,* or *mola mola,* is one of the largest fish in the sea. Its skin, like that of many ocean animals, is often infested with *worms* and other parasites.

The sunfish rises to the *surface* and rolls onto its *side.* The seagull swoops in . . .

. . . and uses its beak to pry *parasites* from the fish's skin.

People sometimes mistake the sunfish's fin for that of a large *shark,* but it's easy to tell the difference. A shark's fin cuts straight through the water, but the peculiar shape of the sunfish's body makes its fin wobble.

The **hippopotamus** spends much of its time in the water . . .

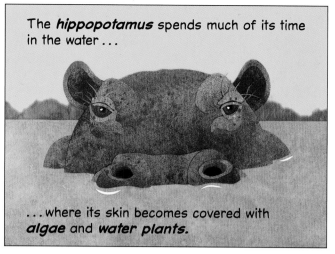

. . . where its skin becomes covered with **algae** and **water plants**.

An **African helmeted turtle** can help.

As in many other cleaning relationships, the hippo holds still while the turtle does its work, **nibbling** away unwanted greenery.

The hippo also lets the cold-blooded turtle use its back as a platform for **basking** in the sun.

The **sea anemone** and the **clownfish,** with its immunity to the anemone's poisonous tentacles, are one of the best-known examples of animal **symbiosis.** But this relationship is more complex than it might appear.

At first, the clownfish isn't immune to the anemone's toxin. It must acquire its resistance by brushing lightly against the **stinging tentacles,** gradually touching them more and more.

The clownfish hides from predators among the anemone's stinging tentacles. It helps the anemone find food by luring **other fish** to their death in the anemone's tentacles.

The clownfish is immune only to its own anemone. If it swims into another anemone — even one of the same kind — it will be **killed.**

If the clownfish leaves its anemone for more than 45 minutes, it will no longer be **safe.** It will have to start over, once again exposing itself gradually to its anemone's stings.

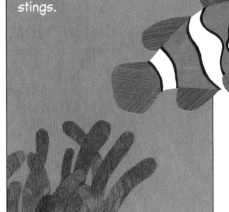

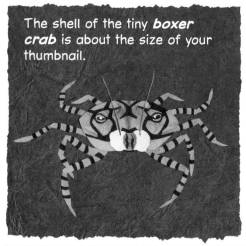

The shell of the tiny **boxer crab** is about the size of your thumbnail.

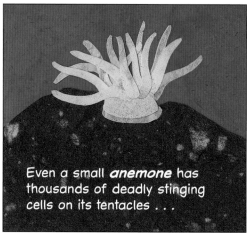

Even a small **anemone** has thousands of deadly stinging cells on its tentacles . . .

. . . but the little crab **plucks** two anemones from the sea floor.

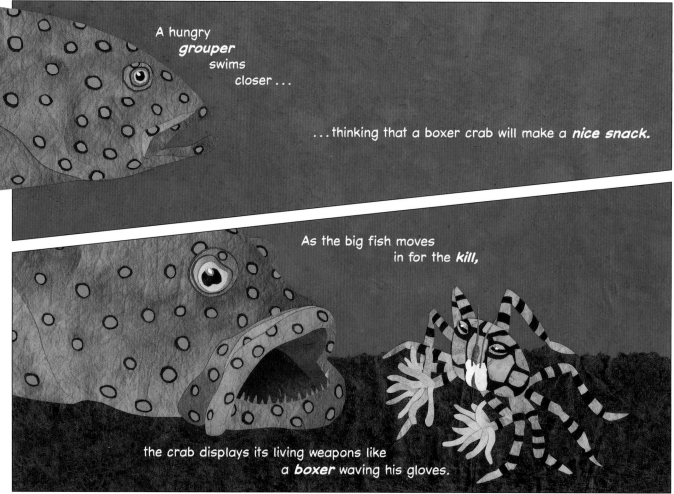

A hungry **grouper** swims closer . . .

. . . thinking that a boxer crab will make a **nice snack.**

As the big fish moves in for the **kill,**

the crab displays its living weapons like a **boxer** waving his gloves.

The grouper decides to look for **easier prey** somewhere else.

Later, when the crab has its own meal, the anemone is rewarded with stray **scraps** of food.

Other crabs also carry living protection and camouflage on their backs. Their passengers get bits of food that drift up as the crabs eat.

The **hermit crab** lives in a shell abandoned by another animal. It tickles an **anemone** with its claws, and the anemone climbs onto the crab's shell. Its **stinging tentacles** protect the crab.

The **sea sponge** isn't poisonous, so it can't defend the **sponge crab** that gives it a ride. But it's hard for a predator to spot a crab with a colorful sponge growing on its back.

With its pincers, the crab keeps the sea sponge **trimmed** to just the right size.

The **decorator crab** adorns its shell with **anemones, sponges,** and bits of **shell** and **seaweed.** It looks like part of the sea floor.

Unlike other animals that live on a crab's shell, the **upside-down jellyfish** is not permanently attached. The jellyfish's stinging tentacles provide protection in return for crab meal **leftovers.**

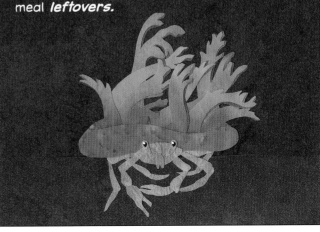

Prairie dogs live in underground colonies. These plump rodents . . .

. . . are one of the coyote's favorite foods.

The badger, an expert burrower, also hunts prairie dogs.

In some places, coyotes and badgers have learned that they can catch more prairie dogs if they hunt together.

The coyote has keen eyesight. It spots a prairie dog colony.

If the coyote attacks, however, a sentry sounds the alarm . . .

. . . and the prairie dogs duck into their underground tunnels.

So instead of rushing in, the coyote sets off to find a badger.

The badger usually hunts alone, but it knows that a coyote can lead it to food. It follows the coyote back to the prairie dog colony.

The prairie dogs spot trouble coming. It's time to *take cover!*

The coyote sniffs out a back entrance to the burrow and waits.

Meanwhile, the badger rips into the burrow entrance with powerful *claws.*

The colony *panics* and the coyote pounces, nabbing one prairie dog as it bolts from a rear exit.

Another darts back into the burrow . . .

. . . straight into the jaws of the waiting badger.

A flock of **ravens** circles overhead. They are following a **wolf pack** that is on the move.

The ravens look on from above as the wolves, working together, attack an **elk.**

Ravens are **thieves.** As soon as the kill is made, they crowd in to steal what they can.

The wolves try to drive the aggressive birds away.

But sometimes the ravens **help** the wolves. If they find a carcass that's too tough for them to eat, they **caw** loudly and more birds arrive on the scene. If wolves hear the call, they come too.

The wolves tear open the carcass, getting a meal for themselves and leaving the leftovers for the ravens.

FOLLOW ME!

A **honeyguide** spies a bee in flight . . .

. . . and trails it back to its **beehive.**

The honeyguide isn't strong enough to break in to the bees' nest, so . . .

. . . it finds a **ratel,** or honey badger, and flutters around it.

The ratel knows that this means **honey.** It follows the honeyguide to the bee's nest.

The honeyguide waits nearby while the ratel tears open the nest and gorges on honey. Its tough skin and thick fur protect it against bee **stings.**

Once the ratel has had its fill, the honeyguide dines on scattered bits of wax **honeycomb** and juicy bee **larvae.**

The sparse hair of the **warthog** does a poor job of protecting its skin from insect **pests.**

Insects filled with warthog blood are a favorite food of the **mongoose.**

An itchy warthog spots a group of mongoose. It **lies down** . . .

. . . signaling the small, catlike mammals. They come **running** . . .

. . . and clamber all over the warthog, which lies quietly while its skin is **picked clean.**

The *marine iguana* is the world's only oceangoing lizard. It lives on the Galápagos Islands...

...where it spends much of its time in the sea, feeding on *algae.*

The water here is *cold,* and the iguana must periodically *warm* its body by lying in the sun.

As it basks, a *Sally Lightfoot crab* takes notice.

Soon this agile land crab is scrambling over the iguana's body. It eats *ticks* and feeds on bits of the lizard's *dead skin.*

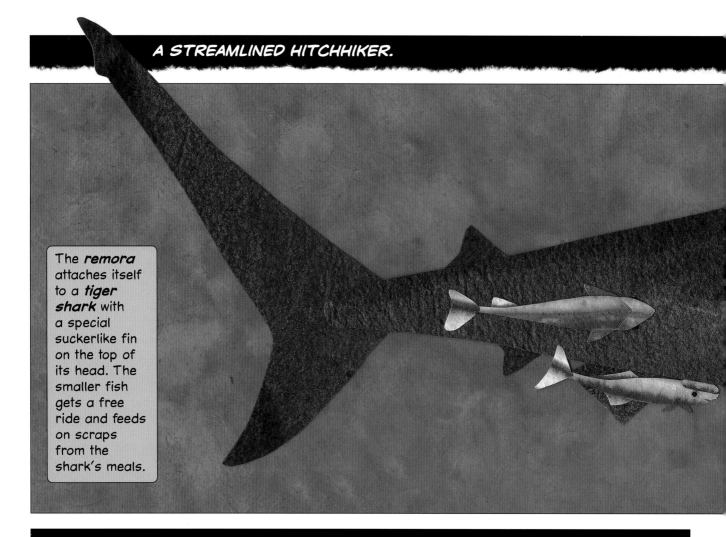

The **remora** attaches itself to a **tiger shark** with a special suckerlike fin on the top of its head. The smaller fish gets a free ride and feeds on scraps from the shark's meals.

CLEANING WHILE YOU WAIT . . .

The **cleaner wrasse** gets its food as it removes parasites from all sorts of sea creatures. These fish gather in a particular spot — a cleaning station — where they service a constant stream of visitors.

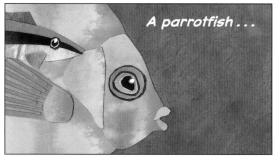

A parrotfish . . .

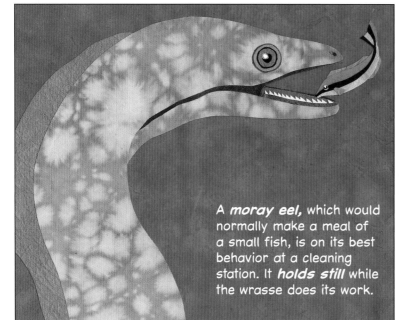

A **moray eel,** which would normally make a meal of a small fish, is on its best behavior at a cleaning station. It **holds still** while the wrasse does its work.

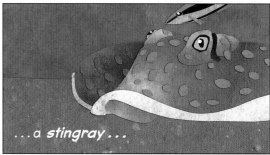

. . . a **stingray** . . .

. . . and a **potato cod** all visit the wrasse **cleaning** station.

The remora helps its host by vacuuming *algae* and *parasites* from the shark's skin.

. . . AND A LITTLE COMPETITION.

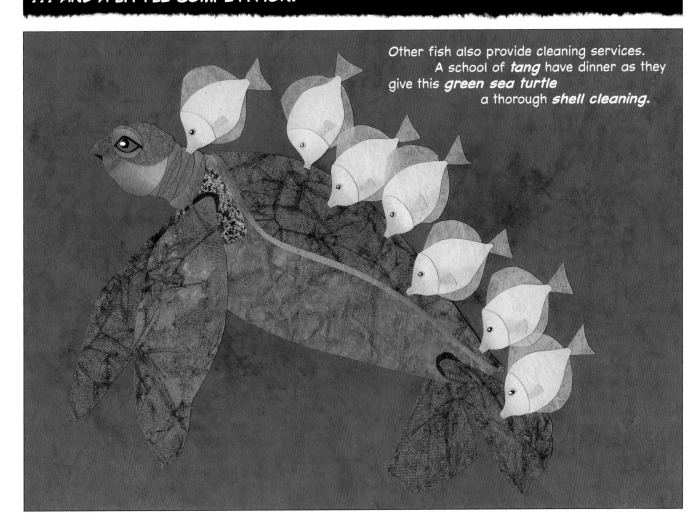

Other fish also provide cleaning services. A school of *tang* have dinner as they give this *green sea turtle* a thorough *shell cleaning.*

The African **social weaver** is a champion nest builder.

Social weaver nests are among the **largest** animal-made structures in the world. As many as 400 birds may live in a single nest. Each family has its own entrance and nesting chamber.

An **African pygmy falcon** moves into the weaver's nest. In many cases, the falcon won't harm the smaller birds. It gets a ready-made home . . .

. . . and helps the weavers by killing **snakes** and reptiles that prey on the small birds or their eggs.

Black tree ants build their nest on a branch high above the ground.

The black ants guard their basketball-sized home fiercely, attacking and **stinging** any animal that comes too close.

The **rufous woodpecker** normally tries to eat the ants, often getting stung in the attempt.

But in the **spring,** when it's time for the female woodpecker to lay her eggs, the situation **changes.**

The bird makes a hole in the nest — a chamber in which she lays her eggs. The ants don't **attack** her, her eggs, or the newly hatched chicks.

The woodpecker doesn't eat the ants, and until the eggs hatch and the baby birds leave the nest, she will help defend it against predators.

Once the **baby birds** leave the ant nest, however, the **ants** and the **rufous woodpecker** become **enemies** once again.

The *tuatara* is an ancient species of reptile that lives in New Zealand.

The tuatara makes its home in the nesting burrows of the *petrel,* a sea bird.

The petrel is active during the **day** and sleeps in its burrow at night.

The tuatara is **nocturnal.** It sleeps during the day and hunts at night.

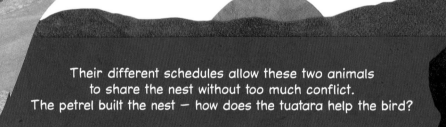

Their different schedules allow these two animals to share the nest without too much conflict. The petrel built the nest — how does the tuatara help the bird?

It **defends** the nest, attacking any animal that threatens the bird or its eggs.

The droppings of the petrel attract **insects, spiders,** and **worms.** The tuatara eats these, keeping the nest **pest-free.**

The **goby** is a small fish that makes its home in cracks, crevices, and holes in the sea floor. It can't dig its own burrow, so it often shares a home with some other creature.

When a **blind shrimp** shares its burrow with a goby . . .

. . . the shrimp uses its antennae to stay in contact, and the fish leads the blind shrimp to **food.**

In case of danger, the goby darts into the burrow. The shrimp **follows.**

Another goby lives with a **pea crab** in a sea floor tunnel excavated by a worm.

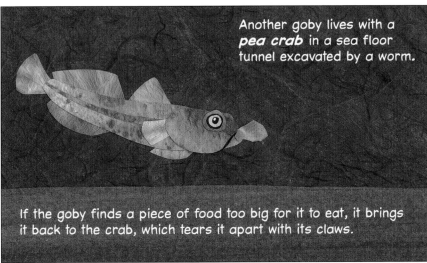

If the goby finds a piece of food too big for it to eat, it brings it back to the crab, which tears it apart with its claws.

Crabs are **messy eaters,** and the goby gets some of the scraps.

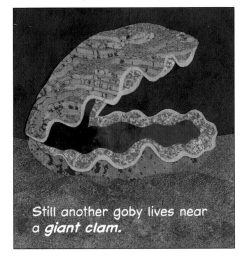

Still another goby lives near a **giant clam.**

If the fish spots danger, it darts into the clam's shell. The clam snaps its shell **shut,** protecting itself and the goby.

After a while, the clam opens its shell a little. If the coast is clear, the goby swims out.

Thousands of **meat ants** live together in underground nests.

During the day the ants leave their nest . . .

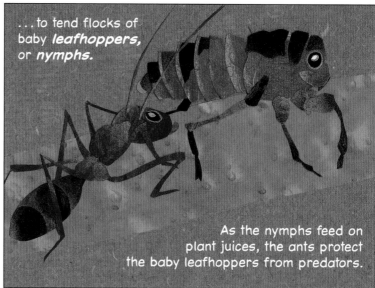

. . . to tend flocks of baby **leafhoppers**, or **nymphs**.

As the nymphs feed on plant juices, the ants protect the baby leafhoppers from predators.

YOU CAN FOOL ALL OF THE ANTS SOME OF THE TIME . . .

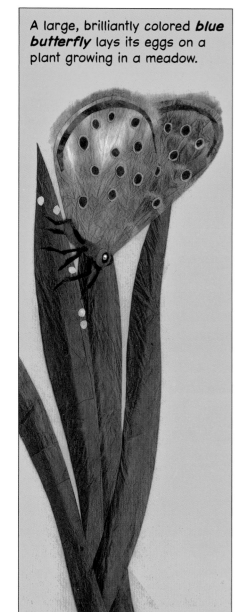

A large, brilliantly colored **blue butterfly** lays its eggs on a plant growing in a meadow.

The egg hatches into a **caterpillar**, which begins to eat the leaves of the plant.

Then the caterpillar does a strange thing. It lets go of the plant and **drops** to the ground.

The meadow floor is a dangerous place for a caterpillar. There are **ants** and other predatory insects everywhere.

Sure enough, a **red ant** soon finds the caterpillar and drags it back to its **nest**.

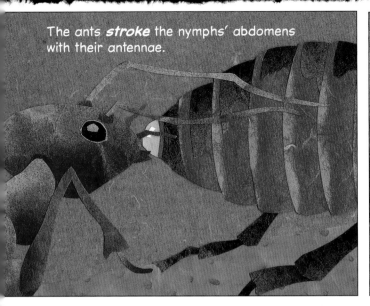

The ants **stroke** the nymphs' abdomens with their antennae.

In response, the nymphs excrete a drop of sweet liquid called **honeydew,** which is the ants' main source of food.

But the caterpillar has a trick: it produces a chemical that smells like an **ant larva.** So instead of **eating** the caterpillar, the ants clean and protect it.

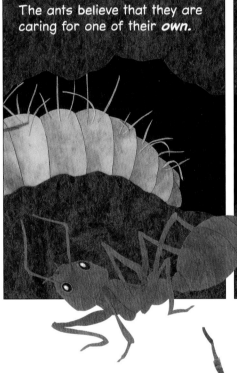

The ants believe that they are caring for one of their **own.**

In return, the caterpillar produces a **sweet liquid,** which the ants drink. The caterpillar eats some of the ant larvae, but the ants don't seem to notice.

Soon, the caterpillar spins a cocoon and becomes a **chrysalis.** It continues to fool the ants by making a **clicking** sound like one the ants themselves make.

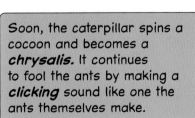

At last the **blue butterfly** emerges from its cocoon. It can no longer fool the ants, and it must leave the nest quickly or be killed by its former caretakers.

Dogs and **humans** have lived together for thousands of years. Their relationship is probably the most commonly observed symbiosis in the animal world.

In return for food and shelter, the first domestic **dogs** — descendants of the wolf — helped **protect** human settlements and livestock.

Today, dogs help humans in many ways:

as workers...

... hunters ...

... herders ...

... and guides.

In return, **humans** feed dogs, provide a home for them, keep them healthy . . .

. . . and give them the **attention** they seem to crave.

Today the most important role for dogs is that of **companion.** Dogs keep us company and cheer us up when we're sad. They are loyal and affectionate.

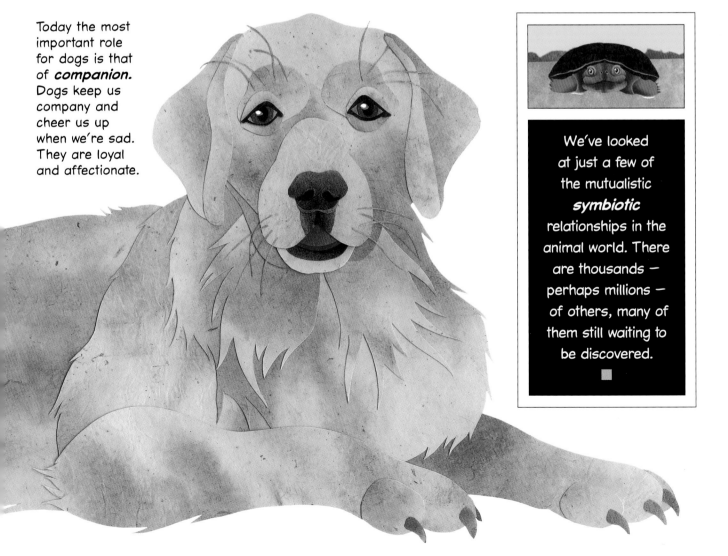

We've looked at just a few of the mutualistic **symbiotic** relationships in the animal world. There are thousands — perhaps millions — of others, many of them still waiting to be discovered.

■

More about symbiosis . . .

There are several different kinds of symbiotic relationships. This book describes *mutualism,* a partnership in which all the animals are helped. There are also relationships in which one animal benefits and another is harmed — a tick and a giraffe, for instance. This is called *parasitism.* A third kind of relationship helps one animal and doesn't hurt or help another. When a barnacle attaches to an oyster's shell, it gets a home, but the oyster isn't really affected. This kind of symbiosis is called *commensualism.*

Sometimes it hard to tell what sort of a symbiotic relationship exists between animals, and scientists don't always agree. For instance, some biologists describe the relationship of the remora and shark as commensualism (the remora benefits, the shark gets nothing). Others believe it is mutualism (that's the way it is described in this book).

Animals don't form mutualistic relationships out of friendship, or from any desire to help each other. They are completely *selfish* and remain in these relationships only because the partnership somehow helps them survive.

Perhaps the most common symbiotic relationships in the world are those between animals and bacteria, such as the one between cows and the microorganisms in their gut that help them digest their food. These relationships are interesting, but difficult to observe and illustrate, so this book focuses on larger organisms.

On these pages you can learn more about the *size, habitat,* and *diet* of the animals in this book.

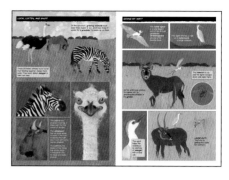

zebra
size: 5 feet (1½ meters) at the shoulder
habitat: African plains and dry grasslands
diet: plants and grasses

wildebeest
size: 4 feet (1¼ meters) at the shoulder
habitat: plains and open woodlands of Africa
diet: short grasses

ostrich
size: up to 9 feet tall (2¾ meters)
habitat: savannahs and dry plains of Africa
diet: seeds, shrubs, grasses, and insects

cattle egret
size: 20 inches (51 centimeters) long
habitat: warm climates throughout the world
diet: grasshoppers, other insects, and frogs

waterbuck
size: 4 feet (1¼ meters) at the shoulder
habitat: savannah and scrublands of Africa
diet: shrubs, tree leaves, and grasses

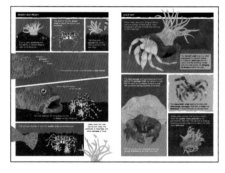

boxer crab
size: ½ inch (1¼ centimeter) across
habitat: Indian and Pacific oceans
diet: plants, dead animals, and zooplankton

hermit crab
size: up to 4 inches (10 centimeters) long
habitat: shallow seas worldwide
diet: plants, worms, and dead animals

sea sponge
size: up to 7 feet (2 meters) tall
habitat: oceans worldwide
diet: small food particles and plankton

decorator crab
size: 5 inches (12½ centimeters) across
habitat: warm ocean shores worldwide
diet: algae, sponges, and small crustaceans

upside-down jellyfish
size: 12 inches (30 centimeters) across
habitat: warm shallow seas
diet: algae and plankton

prairie dog
length: 13 inches (33 centimeters)
habitat: grass prairies and plains of the American West
diet: grasses and insects

coyote
length: 32 inches (81 centimeters)
habitat: throughout North America
diet: small mammals, birds, and reptiles

badger
length: 22 inches (56 centimeters)
habitat: Western North America
diet: rodents and other small animals

raven
length: 25 inches (63.5 centimeters)
habitat: most climates worldwide
diet: fruit, grain, and live and dead animals

wolf
length: up to 6½ feet (2 meters) nose to tail
habitat: northern North America and Asia
diet: small mammals and other animals, deer, elk, and moose

honeyguide
length: 6 inches (15 centimeters)
habitat: forests of Africa and southern Asia
diet: insects, spiders, honeybee larvae, and beeswax

ratel (honey badger)
length: 26 inches (66 centimeters)
habitat: dry grasslands of Africa, India, and Southeast Asia
diet: small mammals and reptiles, birds, eggs, insects, and honey

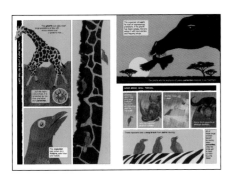

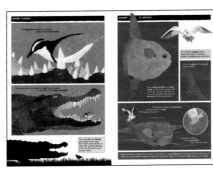

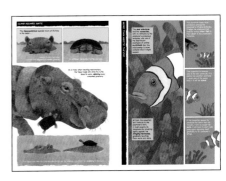

oxpecker
size: 8 inches (20 centimeters) long
habitat: savannahs and forests of Africa
diet: ticks, flies, and blood of host animals

giraffe
size: up to 18 feet (5³/₄ meters) tall
habitat: African savannah and open
  woodlands south of the Sahara
diet: leaves, shrubs, and grass

rhinoceros
size: up to 6,600 pounds (3,000 kilograms)
habitat: African plains and woodlands
diet: leaves, shrubs, and grasses

red deer
size: up to 500 pounds (227 kilograms)
habitat: northern Africa
diet: leaves, shrubs, and grasses

African buffalo
size: up to 2,000 pounds (900 kilograms)
habitat: African plains
diet: leaves, shrubs, and grasses

Egyptian plover
size: 8 inches (20 centimeters) long
habitat: lowland tropical rivers of Africa
diet: insects, worms, and scraps of food in
  crocodiles' teeth

African crocodile
size: up to 20 feet (6 meters) long
habitat: African rivers, freshwater
  marshes, and swamps
diet: fish; zebras, wildebeests, and other
  mammals; birds; and other crocodiles

ocean sunfish (mola mola)
size: 10 feet (3 meters) long, weighs up to
  5,100 pounds (2,300 kilograms)
habitat: temperate and tropical waters of
  oceans worldwide
diet: mainly jellyfish

seagull
size: 20 inches (¹/₂ meter) long
habitat: seacoasts worldwide
diet: fish, shellfish, insects, and worms

hippopotamus
size: up to 4,000 pounds (1,800 kilograms)
habitat: rivers and lakes in Africa
diet: grass and water plants

African helmeted turtle
size: 6 inches (15 centimeters) long
habitat: wet areas throughout Africa
diet: insects, fish, snails, algae, and water
  plants

clownfish
size: 6 inches (15 centimeters) long
habitat: southern Pacific coral reefs
diet: algae, plankton, and undigested food
  from their host anemones

sea anemone
size: 3 feet (91 centimeters) in
  diameter (the anemone associated with
  the clownfish)
habitat: shallow Indo-Pacific Ocean waters
diet: fish, mussels, and zooplankton

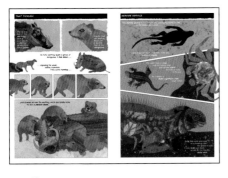

warthog
size: up to 5 feet (1¹/₂ meters) long
habitat: savannahs, woodlands, and
  grasslands of Africa
diet: plants, eggs, small animals, and dead
  animals (carrion)

mongoose
size: 12 inches (30 centimeters) long
habitat: African grasslands and forests
diet: insects, lizards, snakes, and eggs

marine iguana
size: 4 feet (1¹/₄ meters) long
habitat: rocky shores of the Galápagos
  Islands
diet: marine algae

Sally Lightfoot crab
size: 3 inches (7¹/₂ centimeters) across
habitat: warm coasts of the Americas and
  Africa
diet: algae, dead fish and birds, and marine
  iguana parasites and skin

remora
size: 2 feet (60 centimeters) long
habitat: warm ocean waters worldwide
diet: parasites and leftover scraps

tiger shark
size: 13 feet (4 meters) long
habitat: warm coastal waters worldwide
diet: fish, seals, birds, squid, turtles, and
  dolphins

cleaner wrasse
size: 4 inches (10 centimeters) long
habitat: rocky sea floors and coral reefs
diet: the parasites of other fish

tang
size: up to 8 inches (20 centimeters) long
habitat: northern Pacific Ocean
diet: algae and parasites

green sea turtle
size: 5 feet (1¹/₂ meters) long
habitat: warm oceans worldwide
diet: sea plants

social weaver
size: 7 inches (18 centimeters) long
habitat: southern Africa
diet: insects

African pygmy falcon
size: 8 inches (20 centimeters) long
habitat: eastern and southern Africa
diet: insects, small reptiles, and mammals

black tree ants
size: ¹/₆ inch (4 millimeters) long
habitat: trees in the forests of Southeast
  Asia and Africa
diet: plant material

rufous woodpecker
size: 9 inches (23 centimeters) long
habitat: India and Southeast Asia
diet: ants and other insects, fruit, and sap

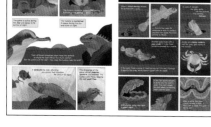

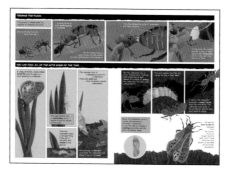

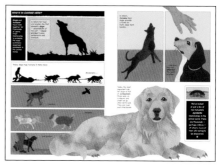

tuatara
size: up to 32 inches (81 centimeters) long
habitat: small islands of New Zealand
diet: earthworms, slugs, and insects

Cook's petrel
size: 11 inches (28 centimeters) long
habitat: sea shores of the Pacific Ocean
diet: fish and shellfish

goby
size: up to 4 inches (10 centimeters) long
habitat: shallow ocean waters worldwide
diet: worms and other small invertebrates

blind shrimp
size: 2 inches (5 centimeters) long
habitat: southern Pacific Ocean coral reefs
diet: plankton and dead animals

pea crab
size: $3/8$ inch (1 centimeter) across
habitat: oceans worldwide
diet: plankton and algae

giant clam
size: 4 feet (122 centimeters) across
habitat: Indo-Pacific ocean
diet: algae

meat ant
size: $3/8$ inch (9 millimeters) long
habitat: throughout Australia
diet: plants and live and dead animals

leafhopper
size: nymph, $1/3$ inch (8 millimeters) long;
  adult, $1/2$ inch (13 millimeters) long
habitat: plants worldwide
diet: plants and plant sap

blue butterfly
size: caterpillar, $1/2$ inch (13 millimeters);
  butterfly, 2-inch (5-centimeter)
  wingspan
habitat: meadows in Europe
caterpillar diet: flowers, then ant larvae
butterfly diet: flower nectar

red ant
size: $1/5$ inch (5 millimeters) long
habitat: central Europe, Asia, and North
  America
diet: insects and honeydew excreted
  by aphids

domestic dog
size: 3 pounds (1,300 grams) to 180 pounds
  (81 kilograms)
habitat: human habitations worldwide
diet: meat and grain, table scraps, and
  small animals

For Page, Alec, and Jamie

Houghton Mifflin Books for Children is an imprint of Houghton Mifflin Harcourt Publishing Company.
www.hmhbooks.com
The text of this book is set in Dave Gibbons Lower. The illustrations are collages of cut and torn paper.

Library of Congress Cataloging-in-Publication Data is on file.
ISBN 978-0-547-24515-7

Printed in Singapore
TWP 10 9 8 7 6 5 4 3 2 1
4500202843

To learn more about animal symbiosis:

Coyote and Badger.
By Bruce Hiscock. Boyds Mills Press, Inc., 2001.

How Animals Live.
By Bernard Stonehouse and Esther Bertram.
Scholastic Reference, 2004.

Perfect Partners.
By John Woodward. Heinemann Library, 2004.

The Usborne World of Animals.
By Susanna Davidson and Mike Unwin.
Usborne Books, 2005.

The Way Nature Works.
By John D. Beazley.
Macmiillan Publishing Company, 1992.

The Wonders of Life on Earth.
By the editors of Time and Lincoln Barnett. Time Inc., 1960.